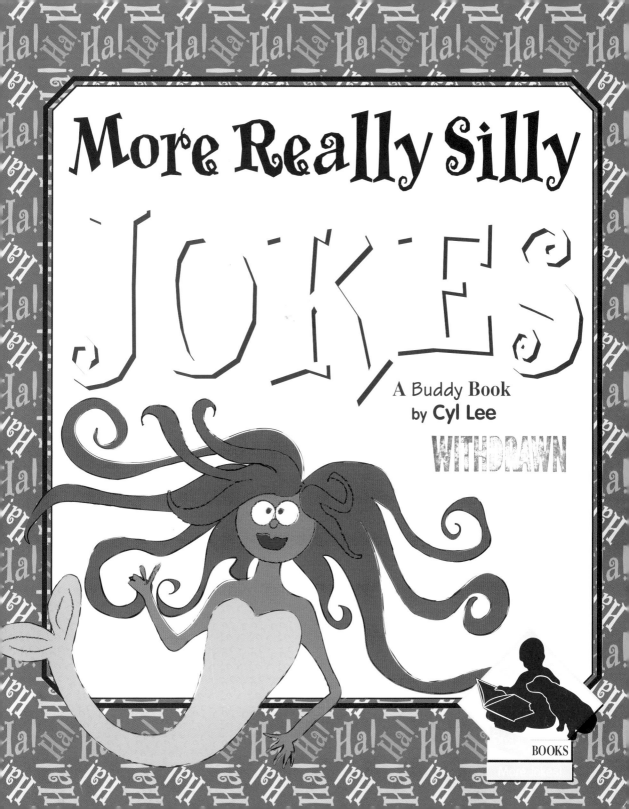

VISIT US AT

www.abdopub.com

Published by ABDO Publishing Company, 4940 Viking Drive, Suite 622, Edina, Minnesota 55435.
Copyright © 2005 by Abdo Consulting Group, Inc. International copyrights reserved in all countries. No
part of this book may be reproduced in any form without written permission from the publisher.

Printed in the United States.

Edited by: Sarah Tieck
Contributing Editors: Jeff Lorge, Michael P. Goecke
Graphic Design: Deborah Coldiron
Illustrations by: Deborah Coldiron and Maria Hosley

Library of Congress Cataloging-in-Publication Data

Lee, Cyl, 1970-
  More really silly jokes / Cyl Lee.
      p. cm. — (More jokes!)
  Includes index.
  ISBN 1-59197-875-0
      1. Wit and humor, Juvenile. I. Title. II. Series.

PN6166.L43 2005
818'.602—dc22

                                                    2004055447

What's the most important thing to learn in chemistry?

Never lick the spoon!

How do you know that Saturn has been married more than once?

Because she has lots of rings!

What did the astronaut say after eating his first meal on the moon?

"The food was good, but the place lacked atmosphere!"

What did the tie say to the hat?

"You go on a head and I'll hang around!"

How did the astronaut serve dinner in outer space?

On flying saucers!

What is a flood?

A river that's too big for its bridges!

Why did the king go to the dentist?

What happens when you throw a green stone in the Red Sea?

Why did the man hit the clock?

Why did the guy run fast?

What keeps jazz musicians on Earth?

Groovity!

What is an archaeologist?

Someone whose career is in ruins!

How does an Eskimo mend
his house?

With i-glue!

What illness do martial artists get?

The kung flu!

How do frogs send messages?

Morse toad!

What do you get if you cross a
four-leaf clover with poison ivy?

A rash of good luck!

9

A man gets a job at the zoo pretending to be a gorilla. On his first day, he puts on his costume and jumps around, beating his chest and roaring. It is fun, until he loses his balance and falls into the lion's cage! The lion roars. He screams, "Help, Help!" The lion races over to him, places his paws on his chest, and hisses,

"Quiet, or we'll both lose our jobs!"

Why did the burglar take a
shower?

He wanted to make a clean
getaway!

Jupiter comes down to Earth one day and decides to help two bank robbers. They get caught and the three of them find themselves in court. Jupiter is a bit shocked when the judge sentences him to 10 years. "I didn't even take part in the robbery," Jupiter says. The judge replies,

"You helped them planet!"

What do you call a country where the people drive only pink cars?

A pink car-nation!

Why don't you ever iron a four-leaf clover?

You might press your luck!

What insect is musical?

A hum-bug!

What do you call it when worms take over the world?

Global worm-ing!

What did the cook give his girlfriend for their anniversary?

A fourteen "carrot" onion ring!

What do mermaids have on toast?

Orange mer-malade!

A group of school children at a museum are studying the dinosaur bones. One of them asks the guard, "Can you tell me how old the dinosaur bones are?" The guard replies, "They are three million, four years, and six months old." The child looks confused. "How do you know that?" he asks. The guard answers, "Well, the dinosaur bones were three million years old when I started working here,

and that was four and a half years ago."

What's the most popular snack on Mars?

Mars-mallows!

Why is a slippery pavement like music?

If you don't C-sharp, you'll B-flat!

Why were the early days of history called the Dark Ages?

Because there were so many knights!

What do you call a hippie's wife?

Mississ-hippie!

What did Delaware?

She wore her New Jersey!

Man: Waiter, this soup tastes funny!

Waiter: Then why aren't you laughing?

Why do firefighters wear red suspenders?

To keep their pants up!

What happened to the passengers when the red and blue ships collided?

They became marooned!

What color is a burp?

Burple!

How does the barber cut the
moon's hair?

Eclipse it!

How did the astronaut serve sodas?

In sun-glasses!

When do astronauts have lunch?

At launch time!

What kind of star wears sunglasses?

A movie star!

Why are chemists great for solving problems?

They have all the solutions!

Web Sites

Visit ABDO Publishing Company on the World Wide Web. Joke Web sites for children are featured on our Book Links page. These links are monitored and updated to provide the silliest information available.

www.abdopub.com